BOOK BENCHERS PUBLICATIONS PRESENTS

TRANSGENDER

Compiled by

S.HARSHANA DEVI

DHARSHINI.M

AELAY PUBLICATION

A dream come true for every writers out there. We spot every possible problem for the writers, help in rectifying them and guide them towards the best outcome. We make sure to understand your needs, dreams and expectations, and nourish them with our services and stop not until we fulfil your dreams. The writers have a right and freedom to choose what they want here. They have us to guide them through the hardest path until the end. Believe in us.

Aelay Publication - by a writer for the writers.

BOOK BENCHERS

Book Benchers is the affiliate of Aelay publication. Both the publication is handled by Astro.
Aelay plays the role of publishing solo books.
And Book Benchers is epically for publishing anthologies.

Book Benchers have 2 different teams.
1. Tamil

2. English/Hindi

Never mind what our main motive is to help all the budding writers, who are seeking for their dream of publishing their own book to come true.

We are there to help out everyone.
In guiding for starting up with your carrier in compiling until finishing up your full book.

COPYRIGHT

(Affiliate by Aelay Publish)

Book: TRANSGENDER
Compiler: S.HARSHANA DEVI
Compiler: DHARSHINI.M
First Edition: October 2021

Published By:

The Book Benchers
5/175, Fathima nagar,
Kuthenkuly,
Tirunelveli -627104
Phone: 9944992571

Design And Executed by

ISBN : 978-93-91423-79-7
Page : 129

ACKNOWLEDGMENT

To list who all have helped us is difficult because they are so numerous and the depth is so enormous. We would like to acknowledge the following as being idealistic channels and fresh dimensions in the completion of this book.

We take this opportunity to thank the Co-authors for being a part of this book and submitting their beautiful writer-ups and making this book more special.

We would like to thank the publication team for providing the necessary facilities required for the completion of this book. We take this opportunity to thank our book editor for the moral support and guidance.

Lastly, We would like to thank every person who directly or indirectly helped me in the completion of the book especially my parents and peers who supported me throughout my book.

DISCLAIMER

This Anthology is a work of fiction. Our editors have tried their best to avoid any sort of plagiarism and the proof-readers have done their job of proofreading best on their part to expertise the book with unplagiarized and original content. Still if any appropriation detected, the editorial team is no where responsible, the author is solely responsible for such acts. We have well guided our co-authors to submit their original write-ups.

TRANSGENDER

FOUNDER

IRUDAGA ASTRO

Irudaga Astro, From Tirunelveli, Founder of
Aelay and BB (Book Benchers)
He had completed his BE.
He has written 3 Tamil poetry book's which
hits the top list on social media!
His main aim is to allow the writers to

publish their words as their book rather than

just Posting them on Insta.

LINK AND POSTER MAKER

CATHERINE ASMI T

Catherine Asmi T, From Tirunelveli
She has completed her M.com
Her passion is Drawing and Designing.

TRANSGENDER

<u>TEAM HEAD</u>

<u>KA. PARINASRI</u>

She is a passionate writer from Chennai. Writing makes her pressure go away. She had played the role of co-author for more than 100+ Antho's. She would like to thank her parents and her Loveable Brother for supporting her rather than stopping her from what she wanted to do! For being the main reason for achieving her dreams. As well as for standing beside her in all the ups and downs. Whenever she feels like she needs to get out of her stressful timing or feels like she needs peacefulness, she starts to paint, she would never mind sitting in the same place for so many hours when it comes to her painting. She believes that anyone could hurt her, But never her books could!!

Catch her in Insta and FB
Insta: @theinnocentheart
FB: KA. PARINASRI

CO – AUTHOR LIST

1. M.Srinithi

2. Kalamkaar

3. Lipsa Dabhi

4. Jebisha

5. Mydeensha

6. SRIJA SADHUKHAN

7. Mohammed Niyaz

8. Banupriya K

9. Iqra Anjum

10. Harikrishna Mynampati

11. Berdhisha P

12. ANKITA NAHAR

13. Vartika Modi

14. Mrithika Manimuthukumar

15. Har Deepansh Bahadur Sinha

16. R. Jeeva Latha

17. Shalini B.S

18. Prathiksha Kumar

19. Mahima Rastogi

20. Harshita verma

21. Kovidha

TRANSGENDER

22. Sujan Dinakar Raktade

23. Kowsika . E

24. Ishvarya shanmugavadivel

25. Deesha Soni

26. Durga Balamadhavan

27. Asbhin Diana P

28. P. Sangareshwari

29. Mahiba

30. Ishwariya

31. M. Pandeeswari

32. Ankita sarkar

33. Shanmugapriya. T

34. K.Manonmani

35. Mohanapriya. K

36. K. Eswari

37. M.Guru Pirabha

38. Riya Richard R L

39. Yachika Prajapati

40. KALAIYARASI.M

41. E. Arun Gnana Mozhi

42. Kevin Pavithren. J

43. Muthu vinnarasi M

44. Balasivanethri Ganesan
45. Soumya . R
46. Raghul Prabakaran
47. I.k . Hemilaa
48. Gnana Sekaran
49. Monisha.k
50. Priya

COMPILER

S.HARSHANA DEVI

Harshana: She is Harshana from Ramanathapuram, Tamil Nadu. She completed her Masters in English. She loves to explore something new. She has more passion in innovating new ideas. She was sportive and humour. She loves to be happy always. She has many friends and love to make new friends. Her dream is to be different.

TRANSGENDER

We are talking about gender inequality

But we never consider about the other gender

In this universe

Male and female is common

But

The most powerful is

Transgender

They are not like us

They are better than us

We never respect them

But

They never disrespect us

That's different between us

Learn to respect them

CO- COMPILER

DHARSHINI.M

She is Dharshini .M from Tamilnadu. She is scholar, completed Masters in English literature . She has huge passion on writing .She is friendly , supportive and energetic young soul . Her friends calls as her as Dharshji .She believe that optimistic thoughts will ensure to lead a great life and wants to spread it through her words that she scribe. She always carries a hope that she will shine soon in her passion .She has participated in many anthologies and She is also successful doing quite few project as complier . She has also published a solo book named 'Vox of mine '.

Insta id ; dharshji_dharsh

NEED A CHANGE

We need a world where human treat with humanity

Not by looks, not by gender

But as human being

Transgender need to be treat equal

Without any differences

The extra two seconds looks on transgender

Made them to feel that you are seen them
differently

We should spread a warm smile rather than stare

They are not stranger; they are stronger to handle
any situation

We should create opportunities and placement

To enhance their lives and rights

Stop judging; start accepting

Respect them and stand with them

To provide great society to live

OUR CO-AUTHOR
&
THIER WRITE-UP

M. SRINITHI

She is srinithi . She completed her master degree in English literature. She is a blogger and budding writer who written many excellent blogs and verse . She is outstanding scholar and talented woman.

Instagram id ; Srinithi_manoharan

LOUD CRY

Transgender, when I hear this word or see them first, come to my mind is living goddess of world. Its not their mistake to turn as transgender, but they leave their family and relatives. They lead their life with more difficulties, Even though they don't have a proper fundamental facilities including bathrooms and toilets. Sometimes we may get confused. Whether we have to address he or she, but they feel Happy while calling them as women. In public places like bus stand, Railway stations we came across them and we easily ignore them. We don't have a single minute to see them. Most of us thought that transgender is, those who clap their hands and get money from men, But we used to Mock them. They override all these obstacles and keep smile in their face. They run their life with low cost of money where they pleading from others. When I feel low think about them and motivated myself and get rid of my sadness. Compared to the their ups and downs in their life Our problem is drop of water in ocean.. When they came near to us, we just move an inch with disgusting. We don't know their inner feelings. Respect them .. They are going to rock the world Throw a small smile!! Smile smile!! towards them.

LIPSA DABHI

She is Author and also good Co-Author. She is eighteen years old, she is student of the computer engineering. She is extraordinary person. She is always good leader. Her mam mrunal prajapati is her inspiration person and also her motivater, her friend chetna raval also supported to her and her mom manisha ben and her father nilesh bhai also supported to her for anytype of her creativity. she also wrote poems, short stories, shayries. Her writing skills almost very well and her creative collections are always best.

Instagram id __lipsa__dabhi__0829

THE TRANSGENDER

1. The transgender is not a wrong,

Because of transgender is one type of god gift for his,

Transgender is one type of medical issue nothing else,

So please understood third gender is same as other genders.

2. Being a transgender,

You are not in the wrong body,

You are not in the wrong journey,

Instead you are in wrong society, who don't understood about of transgender.

3. The transgender ?

Here is nothing to fun and joy,

Respect all they are also sent and created by our god,

Don't shame but understood third gender also.

JEBISHA

Jebisha, a Journalism student. I writes poems and articles that speaks about the social issues. I am working as a co-author in more than thirty anthologies. Writing is my Passion.

Instagram id @jebisha.jebisha.5680

A FEW QUESTIONS

A few questions to the ruthless society :

If he feels feminine himself in his mind, then who are you to dissolve his dreams and assign him away ?

Feminine is not a worst feeling.. It's a beautiful feeling that portraits motherhood. Motherhood doesn't mean that a women gives birth to her baby. The real meaning of motherhood is what , a mother cares everyone as her children with love and care.

We are living in the country, that worships Arthanathiswarar as God. Think of the transgender people who are living among us in the form of that God. Just imagine, how graceful they are?

O! All the parents who thinks to assign their children by listening the wicked talks of the fellow society, I want make you understand, this ruthless society only throw such crushed words on you. Don't hear it and don't make your child feel alone. The society only talks . Only your children will take care of you in your old-age.

" Struggling beyond many embarrassments, now they are standing as achievers along with us. "

Society can't stop them and decide their future,
only they decide the heights they want to reach.

Give them space to grow. They belong to us.

And finally," O! My Dear Society!

Shut down Your empty talks and help them to
improve their quality of life "!

MYDEENSHA

He is Mydeensha. He is an hard working person .
He loves to write his thoughts and love on his
beloved love. He writes to impress her and wanna
make her to feel Special and loved

Instagram id Yuvisha 12

THE TRANSGENDER.

She is an angel,

And other creature of God

I feel the goodness in their blessing

There is no sort of neglect them

They just need to accept them

Nothing else they need from us

I feel painful when they mocked by others

The society is free to accept them as them

Providing opportunity to them

Will surely make their standard high

We should shower respect

And treat them as normal human being.

TRANSGENDER

SRIJA SADHUKHAN

Srija Sadhukhan is 19 years old girl studying BSc Biotechnology in Amity University Kolkata. Love to write poetry and a book worm too.

Instagram id ; Syncopatemysuccess

THE EUNUCH

Struggle of a transgender

Look, laugh and least bothered,

Calling them he or calling them she

As they can live their life

The way they want - stop judging them.

Let them live with their own rights,

They are not weird as defined by our words.

Being a 'transgender' is their choice,

Transgender people are as normal as humans

It's better not to discriminate - respect them.

MOHAMMED NIYAZ

Mohammed Niyaz hails from Mumbai - The City Of Dreams. He often loves to write poetries and short music video stories for his own youtube channel. Apart from this Mohammed is currently working on his upcoming anthologies, as well writing poetries since 2013. You can find him on facebook/mohammed niyaz as well on instagram @niyazsks.

Instagram id ; niyazsks

HUMANITY NEEDS NO GENDER

What if they are different from others.

Aren't they the creations of almighty through mother's.

Though we knew that they can't live in a society like us.

But that doesn't mean they don't have dreams of fuss.

Their dedication needs no fame.

As they have themselves the best of name.

Luck salutes them whenever they wishes something for someone.

When loads of desires touches the rise of none.

They have been always through tough times.

As sarcasm and tantrums became the usual rhymes.

Not once but thrice they have been disrespected by the crowd.

When no one has treated them equally till about.

They have been a lesson from the chapters of enders.

Teaching everyone that "humanity needs no gender".

BANUPRIYA K

She is Banupriya K hails from thoothukudi district. She is currently pursuing secod year post graduate Mathematics. She usually writes a blog.

Instagram id ; banu_k_11

TRANSGENDER

TRANSGENDERS!

I'm Searching to describe yourself, Not at all Poets, Sweet words!

Born as Survivors, But not a wrong person!

Ignore Ignore while Family and Society, Where they will go only they face the Ignore...

While going washroom also they face the Tribulations, Where should go Male toilet Or Female toilet...

Like many Tribulations and Problems you have to face in your daily life cycle...

That Creator's Error is not yours Error!!!

There are struggles in life. But, life is a Struggle in your's life!!!

Ours Society has daily accepting many challenges, Then why it only Refuses to accept the Gender Change?

While giving love She is a Mother, Tags for the Entry He is a Father, and a lovable friend...

While People's seeking himself for help, Nothing putting for himself, and whatever they have they gave these shows that they are the compared to Precious Atchaya Pathiram...

If you asked someone what are you going to become? Many of them answers, I want to become a Doctor, Teacher, lawyer...

But If you asked me, I will definitely tell, I want to become a Good Human.

By Birth we're not Human beings, It comes by Virtue!

We didn't have the Humanity, Then why should we have the Name Human being only?

We are enjoying our Freedom, But they didn't able to enjoy...

What will they want from us?

They expect only love and warmth with us!

TRANSGENDER

IQRA ANJUM

Co-author Iqra Anjum is a juvenile and from the city of pearl's Hyderabad. She is a hostile student and believes that "Hostellers always rock". Being an introvert she adores penning her thoughts. She writes under the pen name of Introvert:)

Instagram id ; introvert6518

TRANSGENDERS ARE SENT BY GOD

Transgenders are not too different as our society makes them feel. Our society always tried to leave them aside.

Don't laugh at them, They are too humans. They just need equality in our society.

They just need acceptance and affection from our society. Respect them, they are similarly sent and created by our God.

HARIKRISHNA MYNAMPATI

He's Harikrishna, working in government sector as a junior assistant. He's a motivational writer, Fitness and Martial arts Enthusiast, and A Charity Volunteer with bachelors in Commerce and the mind of techie. He finds it intresting in solving puzzles and making conversations with new people to explore the beautiful colors of the world.

Instagram id ; @get_set_hkfit

DEAR FRIEND!

The society has named him as sinner,

The companies has made her ineligible,

The studies has become harder for him,

The livelihood has become hell for them...

With some hope on life, cancer patients are living good..

But they're facing hurdles all over their life...

It's hard to get a friend, harder to get life partner...

It's hard to get a shelter, harder to live there...

It's hard to accept their life, harder to accept the society...

Despite the hardships, they're living happily ever after now...

I'm proud of you my friend,

You're the best ever example to live happily in life...

It's not pity we show, but it's concern when you fail...

TRANSGENDER

It's not just showing off, but it's the admiration
when you succeed....

Apart those hurdles you crossed, I'm proud that
you never give up my friend

BERDHISHA P

She is Berdhisha from Coimbatore. She loves to write poetry in Tamil and English. She is a blogger you can read her poems in berdhisha96.blogspot.com .

Instagram id ; thoughts_of_mine_the_muse

RESPECT

God has created the world

God has created the human

Human created the gender

The world respect male and female

But not the transgender

In reality,

They are unique creation of God

The world have to respect them

The world is hurting them

Everyone has to stop that thing

Love them as you love yourself

Respect them as you respect yourself

That's the thing they need.

ANKITA NAHAR

#AKII#@@@ Ankita Nahar, physically she live in AJMER, RAJASTHAN but heartly live in everywhere. She is too much passionate about writing. She have always found comfort in words, and thats what attracts everyone. Writing is her therapy, she write what she feels and experiences in her life. You can take a look at her writings on Instagram @naharankita1

TRANSGENDER

Yes i know

neither are you male

nor are you a woman

but you are not human

who said this

yes i guess

no you the rest

respected as

no respect

but you are a curse

who said this

Yes i know

come uninvited

take thousand rupees

but kills people's rights

who said this

VARTIKA MODI

Vartika Modi is new in writer's feild. She is a student persuing Bba from Teerthankar mahaveer institute of management and technology (TMIMT) and is a huge fan of crime fiction and slasher jounre. She is basically from bhopal. But also she write poetry and is a lowkey shows out her emotions there.

Instagram id ; Ink_it_up_with_me

GENDER EQUALITY

Yeah yeah you heard it right

Gender equality

Girls = Boys

But what about the third one

That ones belong to pride

Why are they not termed as a gender

But as a curse or a demon

No one wants to be with them

But

Everyone wants blessings from them

No one wants to touch them

But

Everyone wants to get them buried in there land

For good luck

Well yes this is

what gender equality is in India

What we want is Girls = Boys = transgender

Yes that's the India we want

MRITHIKA MANIMUTHUKUMAR

She is Mrithika Manimuthukumar residing at Coimbatore, Tamil Nadu.! She has completed her graduation from PSG college of arts and science..!! She is a girl with loads of dreams and is an enthusiastic girl.!! What let's her not sleep is her goal to serve this society and nation by being an civil service aspirant..!! And when it comes to writing, she is a passionate writer who has been an co-author in more than 30+ anthologies and an compiler too.!! She strongly believes that only through words, anything could be changed for the positive.. Words are the most powerful and beautiful blessing in each ones life.. All that takes is to chose to right words.. Your quote : @ Mrithika Manimuthukumar

Instagram id; Mirudikka_Manimuthukumar

TO THE ONE..!!

You are just the way we are

With love is that we adore you

We have assimilated the dreams of you

You are the fossils of your own life

The more you are buried

The more you strive back

Even more stronger and harder than before..!!

Seeing the way you get back on track

Astonishes us that

You are just the way we are..!!

R. JEEVA LATHA

She is a day dreamer. Her names R.Jeeva Latha. She was studying M. Sc physics I yr. Free time writer. Words flowing from her brain that makes her happy.

Instagram id meow_lubb510

THE TRANSGENDER

They are mixture of He and she

Bold and they are emotional

Curse of the hormone

Make them as two

Shirt replaced to saree

They are beautiful angels

And a brave Hero's

We are the reason

For allowing to do illegal works

Their dreams become ashes

Now they are alone

Give them good education

Not money for your lust..

HAR DEEPANSH BAHADUR SINHA

He is Har Deepansh Bahadur Sinha . He belongs to Lucknow,UP. He is a research scholar of Oceanography and has done masters in Geography from National Post Graduate College. Completed his schooling from Study Hall. His hobbies are art , listening to music , cooking & loads of driving. His interest areas are Astronomy, Writing, Photography & Travelling a lot.

Instagram id ; Deepansh_sinha

LET'S ACCEPT & RESPECT

When you look at them so suspiciously

It means you are harming them purposely,

They have also got similar rights

For that you must improve your sight.

What happens if they are transgenders

From our acts they feel like strangers,

The more they work for societies betterment

More than that we hurt their sentiments.

What we do is complete partiality

What they suffer is deep inequality,

We just don't want to accept this clarity

That they have got a unique identity.

Doesn't matter whether they are transgender,
lesbian or gay

It's their life and just let them slay.

SHALINI.B.S

Shalini.B.S is a literature student. Her writing style are about the real feeling,simple and understanding and joyful. She is writing in the pen name of TARA'. Most of her works are based on real life she loves to listen music and interested in drawing and painting.

Instagram id; Kuttyma2611

UNFAIR RESTRICTIONS OF WORLD

I will listen to you,

I will truly listen to you;

But help me with an answer to this

– am I a human?

I must be too complex,

But we share the same language

And also the same world,

I am secluded, sometimes, always;

I could be an artist, you know

Or maybe a great physician

Or maybe a soulful singer.

But I am tired of not being a part,

A part of the unison world.

Do we not see the same sun rise?

Why does not the sun rise for me?

I step back from this time lapse

And wonder how could I not be a human?

My world falls apart when I am frequent reminded

That I must not be made to belong in a world of
two's for I am the third.

MAHIMA RASTOGI

Mahima Rastogi, persuing Bachelor Of Technology From RAJA Balwant Singh Engineering Technical Campus Bichpuri, Agra.She belongs to Rampur which is famous for it's knives"Rampuri Chaku".She is a girl who enjoy every moment of life. She is a nature's lover and also love travelling. She usually writes her thoughts on paper in her leisure time. She believes in simple living high thinking.

Instagram id ; Mahi.marastogi

RESPECT TRANSGENDERS

We are not different from you all

We are also the children of God as you all.

We are the humans

We are also the creation of god.

We gives you blessings

But why we never get them back.

We spread love amongst all

But why we only receives hatred by all.

We transgenders are also the part of society

But why this society doesn't accept us as a part of
society.

We are not same as u all but that's not our fault

But why we don't get the same respect that's all
your fault.

PRATHIKSHA KUMAR

A little girl who lives in her dreams and tries to achieve it in real life. Criminologist, speaker, and lover of writing. Her lines speak about the pain

Instagram id; @prathik_quotes

REAL FIGHTERS

Here is another person's right to do whatever he
likes,

Yes the society that accepts all this,

And call them a wise men and women,

But we respect our physical feelings

And we changed our identity as transgender!

What is the reason for ignoring us alone?

We are the real fighters and we don't want to give
up anymore.

HARSHITA VERMA

Co-author Harshita Verma is a writer from Lucknow. She has completed her graduation in commerce stream. She has been writing poetry for the last few years as her passion. She wants to be a novelist in future.

Instagram id ; 0___hsh

HUMAN

Different from the rest

Still human form in its best

Deserving equal rights and respect

The transgender should not be put to test.

Sharing the same feelings as us

The society judges they don't make a fuss

Try to understand them as humans

Give them their rights to live freely.

Support them as a form of humanity

They deserve love as a community

Break the chain of inequality with them

Share and enjoy the happiness of life with them.

KOVIDHA

Kovidha hails from Hyderabad, Telangana.. She like to decorate her words and emotions on paper and has participated in various anthologies..Additionally, She wants to be unique! to stand out amongst the people and like to learn new things. She believes in delivering smiles on the faces. u can find her writings in IG as evil_dweller585

Instagram id ; Evil_dweller585

GENDER DISCRIMINATION

Where she wishes to thrash, she glides across the
floor.

A puppet bound by the hands of society, pushing,
pushing

To free herself, to change what being a woman
means,

what (gender) equality means.

The man, he is to castrated by the hands to be a
MAN.

What does that mean? Better put, what does that
mean to society?

strip us down, wash away our skin, we are bare,
we are the same,

INSIDE

What makes us, us?

Is it our gender?

Is it society?

No, what makes us, what makes you, is ultimately
your decision,

and thats something, not even society, can take
away from you."

SUJAN DINAKAR RAKTADE

Sujan Dinakar Raktade alias Jayraj is Engineering Student who writes motivational quotes and articles since last 3 years and delivers motivational lectures too.

Instagram id ;mad_jay03

THEY ARE HUMAN TOO

Yesterday I was watching a video on YouTube. I got suggestions about lots of videos and accidently I played one of them. I was quite shocked after watching that video. I don't even believe that we are living in 21st century. That video was about transgender. I was shocked because how much myths still we have about them. In 21st century we are talking about innovations, technologies and all stuff but it was quite disappointing the way we are treating transgender.

Most of us have seen them begging near the traffic signal or in the train but We often ignore or don't even realize is that directly or indirectly we, as a society , are responsible for their condition. After being disowned by their family its our moral responsibility to support them. The lack of education and career opportunities forces then to beg. Earlier days condition was worst than today. Now a days they are getting opportunity of education, jobs and many more things. Its quite positive picture for our society still this change may take some decades but I am sure that one day everything will change.

Scientifically they are little-bit different from average people but still they are humans too. They have right to enjoy the life, experience the freedom but we can encourage them for that. Whenever we will start to treat them as average people they will start to consider themselves as average human being and that day we can make to feel that 'Yes.. Your existence is matters in society...'

KOWSIKA E

Kousika Moorthi, She's a Literature Graduate currently living in Coimbatore. She had a great interest in writing from her childhood. From then till now she never stopped her imagination towards writing. She'll write about the things which affect her more and transfer her Imagination into precious words.

Instagram id ; solitary_diary_

THE ANGELIC BOLD

There's a lot of things are there in this world to
protest against

Think of a person who needs to protest for their
body that belongs to them

Women are compared as Angels,

Men are compared to a bold beast,

But only two genders are there in the world??

What about the transgender,

Why should we segregate them from usual things,

we do not give any powers to do that, are we?

Who are we to accept them that too in broad mind

They are humans as like everyone here,

No one needs to give special importance to them
just respect them what they are

That's the biggest rightness you're doing to them.

ISHVARYA
SHANMUGAVADIVEL

ISHVARYA SHANMUGAVADIVEL is a Mechanical Engineer. She is interested in story writing and also had great interest in reading novels. Her poetry knowledge was good which was inspired by song lyrics in movies. First, she started listening to them. Then on admiring them she began to write. Later it became a passion for her to write. She creates crazy things through her words in writing. She'll convert her imagination into soulfull stories without any considerable change.

Instagram username ; ishvarya_shanmugavadivel

BE PROUD TO BE A TRANSGENDER

Gender is not determine who you are

It's just a biological thing

That's not the administrator of yourself

Beyond society's point

You should know your worth of organismality

In this world has insane on uniqueness,

But they refuse you as especial

Don't mind them to your way!

Everyone has individuality

Know yourself idiosyncratic

Don't blame others for your idle state

You can do what you wish

Prove yourself to you

Achieve the height of work fields !

DEESHA SONI

Deesha Soni..a Post Graduate and M.phil adorns the hat of a multitasker of an educationist,artist,poet,photographer,author , blogger,homemaker,wife and mother... She has 10 years experience in the field of Education as a Professor and Coordinator.Deesha has various publications to her credit in national and international levels. Deesha has various published works to her credit... she has two books published on Amazon... named 'Just thoughts' and 'Random thoughts on pandemic'..Kindle edition and more than 100 plus published works on various online platforms of .. Deesha has been twice nominated for Author of a week award by Storymirror and has also won various recognitions in penning stories and write-ups.. at National and International levels... Deesha has various published works to her credit... she has two books published on Amazon... named 'Just thoughts' and 'Random thoughts on pandemic'..Kindle edition has also won many prizes in National and international levels in many write-ups... Deesha has also published her works in 300 plus anthologies of multiple genres...

Instagram id ; Deeshagaure

TRANSGENDER

Born different....

Born distinct and different are they...

People address them in a different way...

All they want is some respect...

Towards them society should change their
perspect...

A class apart are the other genders..

Sadly they are harassed by offenders...

It's not their fault... that different they are born...

Fair rights...and equality on them should be
showered upon...

Be sensitive to transgenders don't mock or insult
them....

They too have reached heights in varied fields....at
heart they are a gem...

Born different...but they are humans ...

To bless infant after birth...they are the ones....

KALAMKAAR

This is kalamkaar. He is from Uttrakhand bought up in Meerut(Up). His hobbies are reading and writing. His interest is in writing. He love writing. He is part of 860+ Anthologies as Co-Author. He won 730+ Certificate in Writing. He is simple and people observer. His insta handle is kalamkaar51 and email is kalamkaar51@gmail.com. He believes in Karma.

Instagram id ; Kalamkaar51

TRANSGENDER

The people of the world do not adopt them. But after going home these prayers are offered. These are forms of Shiva Shakti, but many are their forms. Why are people away from them, why can't they respect them? If we were one of us, we have a relationship, if we have a relationship with them, then they also have to do it. This is a boon of God, why do people want to live with happiness, they are unaware. Never hurt your heart, you will not be able to escape from their bullshit. You will not find any way to escape, you will find them there. They would have been very beautiful in their mind, they also cry in sorrow. Don't torture them or treat them away Respect them too, neither slander them nor insult them. They are also children of God, I don't understand why they are equal. Every day they have to fight with society They have to fight with themselves to make their own identity. Let's see the smile on their face, no one understands the pain inside their mind. He runs away from them in order to rid them. What sin did he commit by taking the birth of a transgender? Do not give them respect and understand why they are cursed. They also have the right to live in the society. Can do this, should not do anything, there is a doubt on them. He is also one of us, he too has a noble heart. Why does their family leave their side. And why do they have to bear the reproach Give them jobs and all the facilities so that they can stand on their feet. And for being ashamed again and again, don't go to this house again and again to ask for congratulations Live your life with peace and dignity Adopt the society and become a participant in social reform by taking them step by step. spread your black light Those festivals and people also came to their homes to meet them.

DURGA BALAMADHAVAN

Durga Balamadhavan is a self-constructed writer hailing from land of heritage & culture, Tamilnadu. She has been writing poetry & short stories since 3 months as her passion. She has completed her 12 th grade in science stream. She's interested in music, creative writing, dance, drawing & painting & reading books. She loves to tender help to people & contribute to her society. She holds millions of dreams in her heart & working for it day by day. At present she's offering writing & designing services under her own "Uniquedreamer Enterprises" at a very low charge than ever before. Ig handle: @uniquedreamerdurga

EQUAL RIGHTS TO TRANSGENDERS

We speak of gender equality for men & women now-a-days. But where did Transgenders' equality go? Look!! They're also humans & they too get equal rights. Right from the government reservation to the respect, people got to understand their feelings & act accordingly. Now a days, transgenders are imprinting their footprints in various fields like education, sports, social service etc. Many superfemales are now positioned as higher authorities & being the best inspiration to many. So, it's the core responsibility of every individual across the world to ensure the rights of transgenders

P. SANGARESHWARI

She was born in the soil where Karmaveer was born. Her name is Sangareshwari. Social service activist. Many orphans and disabled children have benefited from her. And planted a lot of saplings in this community. She did his bachelor's degree in English but is more interested in Tamil. She is good at writing a lot of stories and poems. She wants to become IAS. Her strength Hope. What she often says is that one day I will definitely become an IAS officer.

Instagram id ; littleprincess2904

TRANS REFUGEE

Stop being confused

Stop being surprised

Stop calling us He or It

We hate that pronoun

We are females we as others

We deserve our rights like others

We deserve love and affection

We deserve Respect like others

We are tired of your nicknames

"Is a he or a she", "what is this?"

It hurts please stop stop stop!

We are fine ladies! Full stop !

You scared our fellow ladies

They are crying in closet

They are lonely in families

Because we are Transgenders!

Stop abusing my brothers

TRANSGENDER

They men and so proud to be

Don't be confused by what you see

A transMan is a powerful Man!

Respect them now and forever

ASBHIN DIANA P

Asbhin Diana from Tamilnadu. She completed her master's degree from Chennai. She loves writing article and poetry

Instagram id ; asbhindiana

HOPE OF LIFE

I met you on local train,

You life made my heart drain,

You deserve a better life,

Not the one filled with strife.

Some of you are educated,

Where as others are being harassed,

Asking for alms was the only choice left,

But you leave the person who give them blessed.

Your appearance many not be friendly,

But most of you are very kind,

Days will go on, change will come,

You too have happy days to come.

M.MAHIBA

Mahiba was a girl studing 9th in kra , she was a brave girl and lion hearted girl she likes to write stories, poem and quotes A woman with dream to become women with vision wants to be Mahiba

Instagram id ; Mahiba

HARD WORK NEVER FAILS

Once upon a time there was was a girl name Manju. She was transgender women. She live with her mother. Her father was a shopkeeper. Her father will always scold and beat her for her birth. By hearing her father's words manju was upset. Then she was praying to god that why her father were always angry on her. Manju aim is to become a doctor. Her mother was helping Manju for her studies. In her coaching center her hear by friend doesn't like manju. She doesn't like to study with manju. So she complained wrong about manju. So they removed manju from the center. Manju did hear anyone word, after hearing this complain she become more interested in her studies. After some days her exam is going to start. In her exam also thay gave more pressure to manju, but manju did stop her exam. Her father was had fell down from the terrace. So they need money for the operation, her mother gave her every jewellery for the operation. They need money for her father's medicine. Finally this was the day manju want to prove her. She went to see her result manju got the state rank in the exam and she got the job. And she started to support her family. And her father asked sorry to manju for beating. And her father said to everyone that he is very proud of manju.
Thank you
HARDWORK NEVER FAILS

M. AISWARYA

She is Aiswarya ,born to Mr.Murugan and Mrs.karpagavali murugan ,hails from Tamilnadu. She is pursuing B. Ed in teacher training and also completed Bachelor in English. She is trained teacher with good knowledge. She loves to read and shares her view of books to her friends. She now turns to budding writer.

TRANSGENDER-RESPECTABLE
UNIQUE

Transgender ,the name itself reveal,
They are unique

Their heart filled up with unwanted thoughts,
Because of us

We have to make them to feel them as usuall
human,
From our attitude towards them

Yes,we only responsible for their sufferings
Because we give more pain from our attitude at
them

Refuse partiality,
Recover freedom.

M. PANDEESWARI

Ms.M.Pandeeswari, PG Scholar, Social Activist and the Bundle of talents hails from Sattur in Virudhunagar district! She have a keen interest in writing. She was awarded much more for her best perks since her Undergraduate. The eternal love between herself and writing was tied up in 2015. Her pen name is கவிதைக் கி(ரு)றுக்கி. She worked as a coauthor in 27+ Anthologies.Her themes: Nature, Motivation, Feminism, and Love.

THE THIRD WINGS...!

Yes, They're third wings..

Bliss of gender community!

Untold laments clenched with their wings..

Pain bearers and living angels!

They're kicked out from their nest..

The society spitting aversion..

Their unsung emotions were suppressed!

They got married and...

They sung lullaby for fantasy children!

But they're too strong...

Men can be a men and

Women can be a woman..

But they're third wings from heaven!

Stars in earth with hope

ANKITA SARKAR

Ankita Sarkar is a girl from Jamshedpur. She did her graduation on Hospitality Management and now majoring in Child Psychology. She has published her own book and has been a part of many anthology books. She express her feelings through words.

Instagram username ; ankitasarkar_4

TRANSGENDER

Transgenders are not sin,

They are shaped by the god,

Who deserves to get respected

And dignity,

That is why their blessings

Are too powerful.

SHANMMUGAPRIYA.T

ShanmugaPriya.T grew up in Madurai,Tamilnadu,India.She is fledgling Aviator studied in Coimbatore . Her target is seeking sow to stand in aviation field. She has vast fascination pouring out her thoughts into verbal. And she believes best companion and true ones are dogs & books. Rather than exhibiting, she prefers inking. She's aspiring writer and Looking forwards for platforms.

Instagram id ; _ukiyo_ame_

GLIMMER GENDER

You types of people are isolated,

Moreover most of all humiliated.

Labelling you in such undignified well

Despite all, you weren't recognized not even as
living mortal .

Because you're the root cause to make it happen

Rather indulging yourself as everybody thinks
you're fit in ditch, Slightly chin up and look
around,

There are many numerous amenities scattered
around.

Since you're Trans ,you're habitat to be crouch
narrowed,

And results everybody is gonna subjugated you.

Rights is not to be served , but it is to be taken by
you.

Choke-out all lamentable tags on you and be on
tenacity none can reach your altitude.

You're totally glimmer unique among all human
being.

K. MANONMANI

She is Manonmani from Tamilnadu. She has completed Bachelor in English and also B.Ed. Now she is doing Masters in English. She is trained teacher with good knowledge. She loves to read and shares her view of books to her friends. She now turns to budding writer.

Instagram id ; Manokarthika_03

TRANS GEN(WON)DER

Everyone rejoiced the moment he was born.

His family serves sweets to everyone.

But nobody knows when he was born,

That he was born with a lie.

He feels something change within him.

He gradually realizes that he is changing.

He just want to be a woman,

And finally he turns him into a woman.

In his young age, everyone hated him,

Society didn't let him be a normal human being.

He finds it very difficult to live in this society.

He fights for his rights till death.

MOHANAPRIYA.K

Mohanapriya.K is a budding writer from Tamilnadu, India. She has completed her Bachelor's degree in Engineering stream. She has been a writer for one year as her passion. She wants to be a best compiler and voice over artist in future. She has been co-author of 210 anthologies so far and worked in many record holding, internationally published anthologies and magazines. She participated in many writing contests on instagram and received certificates. Yet she sincerely hope that this writing journey of her will continue as sweetly as it is now and will bring her many successes. You can find her writings on her instagram page. Instagram : @colours_honey_official E-mail : doraa.kutty@gmail.com

BEING THIRD GENDER DOES NOT MEAN INCOMPETENT.

What we call the third gender is that their world is separate. But none of them wanted to live in a separate world. They just want everyone to live together like normal human beings. But many of us who claim to be ordinary human beings do not see them as ordinary human beings and do not live like ordinary human beings. In fact, those who claim to be normal human beings are more offensive to others than the so-called third gender. In Hinduism, women are considered as Parvati and men as Shiva. Similarly, both man and woman are united in one man and are called "Arthanathisvara". This is the name of the combined image of Shiva and Parvati. This is the incarnation that God took to make it clear that both sexes are always equal except that men and women are physically different. But this society often does not even consider third genders as fellow human beings. Those who were born in their home do not want to be with them in this society from the age of their character. That is why they are separate from everyone else and all those who are like them live together. The best festival they celebrate is the "Kuttandavar Temple Festival". Third genders are not given equal rights in any field. They are denied all the rights they have despite their abilities due to their gender. Is this all fair? All of these are for me Certainly not fair. My desire is that opportunities should be provided to everyone in all fields based on talent and not on gender. Those who set aside the third gender in the past have now achieved much. My heartfelt congratulations to them!

K. ESWARI

Miss K.Eswari from virudhunagar. Completed Bachelor of Arts (B.A.English) at V.V.Vannia perumal college virudhunagar and doing Bachelor of Education (B.Ed) in Srividya college of Education under (TNTEU). Awsome motivational speaker.Great optimistic person.Her way of describing words are very much optimistic.It is her poem. Hope you like her poem. Love her writings very much.In addition,she is interested in drawing. A nice singer and a awsome cook. She is one of my best inspiration.A good supporter. Hope she become a great realistic writer in future. A simple girl with lots of dream.Her Passion is from Miss.K. Eswari to Dr. Miss/Mrs. K. Eswari. Do follow and her on crazythoughtsofficial @insta G.mail:eswarikumaran5@gmail.com

Insta:eswarikumaran2311

Crazythoughts official

THE QUEEN...

Crowned prince of their castle !

Angels from the beautiful heaven !

Pure love in the world of conspiracy!

Awesome warrior of inferiority !

Powerful achievers of future !

Wonderful re-creators of emotions !

Mighty law creators of society !

Immortal warriors of humanity !

Awesome saints of loyalty !

Uncrowned queen of royalty !

Finally they are crowned as a

Princess in the immortal world of love!!!

M.GURU PIRABHA

She is a people's person and love meeting new people and learning about their lives and their backgrounds. She likes making people feel comfortable in her presence.

Instagram id ; crazieeguru

TRANSGENDER

'He' is for third person male gender.

'She' is for third person female gender.

'It' is the third person neutral gender.

What is for third person transgender?

Is that person Sir or Madam?

Is that person Mr., Mrs., or Miss.?

I can see clearly

The world is changing,

Drifting, rearranging

There is only one answer

That is HUMANITY

Being human

In the first place

With dignity and grace

Do not corner

Each other into misery

RIYA RICHARD R L

Riya Richard R. L is a young, burgeoning writer in English. She loves writing from her girlhood. Her passion and desire for writing help her to perform conscientiously. She has a unique style and distinct modus operandi in her writings. She has written more than forty anthologies.

Instagram ID ; rl.riya21

TACKLING THE TRIBULATION

Transgender; one without oddity,

The Only one with both potentiality,

Brave and Strength like Masculine,

Tolerance and Tender like Feminine,

Who is ignored unethically,

Who is abandoned purposely,

This Scenario needs a change

Immediately in every Range,

They deserve respect and right

We must stand by and fight,

To give them a better life,

And eradicate all their strife.

YACHIKA PRAJAPATI

I m Yachika Prajapati from Devbhoomi Haridwar Uttarakhand. I m pursuing my Bcom. And i like writing poetrys and books reading.. I m Poetess by Heart and and entrepreneur by choice.. I want to become a social servant and a Gud Motivational Leader. I love helping people specially job seekers. I have also worked with many anthologies.

Instagram id ; hidden_person_26

GENDER INEQUALITY

In today's era, as human beings are progressing towards progress.

In the same way, he is forgetting humanity.

We talk a lot that everyone has been given equal rights.

But the truth is that there is no such thing.

Here humans hate humans, that too on different grounds.

Earlier there was a distinction between a boy and a girl.

Today we have not been able to eliminate it, we have taken another new disease of dirty thinking.

Gender inequality by which the society suffers badly.

We have started to discriminate on the basis of gender even more now, humanity has been lost.

Do you know that there is something in all of you who are not different to human beings, just cannot express themselves like that when everyone is like that.

Because of us people, they cannot even breathe peacefully.

Nor are they able to feel the peace that they should get.

TRANSGENDER

This society has given them a different identity,
but did not accept them from the heart.

They also have the right as we all have the right to
enjoy the season of celebrating the happiness of
living.

They have nothing, then if they are rejected from
the society.

Like a new dawn, we have to treat them the same
way that we treat each other.

They also need love, they need loved ones in
happiness.

Looking for that shoulder in sorrow on which he
can cry by keeping his head.

M.KALAIYARASI

M.Kalaiyarasi, M.com graduate & TNPSC activist. She express her feelings along with beautiful words and composes her poetry with love.

Instagram id ; @keladi_n_kannammah.tvl

TRANSGENDER

If you have enough money,

to enjoy your life....

Give them a small amount

to improve themselves,

as your family member!

If you have good presence of mind,

to celebrate yourself....

Talk with them,

with unconditional love!

If you have enough friends,

to share your mindset....

Be a good friend to them,

and make them feel comfortable!

They also have Love, Pain, Feelings

like me and you,,,

Let us all respect them as

human shivasakthi, appearance!

There is no shiva,without sakthi!

There is no sakthi, without shiva!!

E. ARUN GNANA MOZHI

She is Arun Gnana Mozhi hails from kovilpatti . She is pursuing B. Ed in teacher training and also completed Bachelor in English. She is trained teacher with good knowledge. She loves to read and shares her view of books to her friends. She now turns to budding writer.

TRANSGENDER

Transgender is just a gender category like men and women.

They don't feel "we are different from the normal people".

But we only make them to feel "they are different".

They don't need any honour from us.

They only need the 'equal respect from us'.

They don't need any support from us.

They just want 'don't make any barriers from their way'.

They feel for everyone emotions and care all

But no one there for their emotions.

Apart from the gender discrimination we are 'humans'.

MUTHU VINNARASI M

Muthu vinnarasi has completed UG. And here she
shares her thoughts

Instagram id ; Vinnarasi6999

HUMANITY

When I was studying in college. I used to go to college by bus.

On that day I was so tired and felt feverish..

So I bought tea and sit inside the bus.

while drinking that tea, there came a transgender.

She asked me "In this hot evening why you are drinking tea?"

And I told her that I was feeling tired.

Without asking me she bought me a tablets and gave me.

There I could see humanity

I couldn't forget this incident forever.

KEVIN PAVITHREN. K

He is Kevin Pavithren. J from Salem, Tamilnadu who finished his Under Graduation in Loyola college of arts and science Mettala. Now he is doing his Post Graduation in Government college of arts and science salem-7. He started his career as a speaker and he has participated in many speech competitions both in Tamil and English. He also participated in a photography competition and won an international certificate. He had published his poetry in Tamil so he won a state level award as best poet in the field of poetry. He is not only an author but also a volleyball player . He also got "Thai ullam Award -2021" for doing excellence is the language tamil. He won third place in National level Poetry competition, Tamil. Kevin got "Kamarajarin Sikaram award "for doing great things. He is also a record breaker in the field of modeling. He is a co - author in the book named INCARNATION. Which is the world largest anthology which has 1409 co- authors. He believes that writing can change the entire world. Now he is doing many short stories, articles, poems, books etc.

Instagram id ; urstrulykevin

RESPECT THEM EQUALLY.

Respect them equally,

Ebbing strength will teach you generosity,

Dabbing them is not a sin!

Naffing by seeing them is a sin.

Earthy particals all are same,

Gender division is just for name,

Slapping the struggles,

Nabbing them as a bundle,

Acrossing everyday's challenge,

Realising the plunge,

They will move through their work.

BALASIVANETHRI GANESAN

Balasivanethri Ganesan is from Salem, Tamilnadu. She did Undergraduate English Literature in Government Arts College for Women, Salem-8 and she is now pursuing M.A English Literature in Government College of Arts and Science, Salem-7. She has faith in her Will Power, Endeavour and Hardwork. She believes in her writings and she wants to fight for justice through her pen. Now she is writing short stories, articles and poems. She is a co author of the book Incarnation, which is the world's largest anthology with 1409 writers.

Instagram id ; @sivanethri

BLURRED IDOLS

We're not men or a women,

But a human!

Is physic important?

More than our intent!

Society ignored us,

Some fools taunting us,

Some demons using us as prostitutes,

Our parents abandoned us and we didn't see
educational institutes!!

Some feel awkward to interact,

It create lot of impact!

Don't seclude us,

Let us live don't cuss!!

SOUMYA R

She is Soumya and a well graduated girl.She used to sing in her leisure times and she loves to travel alone.

Instagram id ; soumiii_____

TRANSGENDER

Yet, like all other human beings, trans people also
have all fundamental rights.

But they constantly face denial and rejection.

Trans people who express their gender are often
rejected by their families.

Unemployment and low paying for high works led
into poverty and homelessness.

From earlier times to till now, they are facing
many sexual harassments.

Trans individuals should be treated as equal as
human beings.

All are equal in the eyes of God.

So give love and respect all.

TRANSGENDER

RAGHUL PRABAKARAN

Raghul Prabakaran is a 20years old budding writer who runs to reach a wholehearted peak in writing career love all the art and dreams through his eyes his principles are love all the creetures in the world and ignore negativity.

Instagram id ; WRITER RAGHUL

BE A MIRROR OF YOURS

In a college a group of boys went to a sports meet and they participate in football competition and they stay for two days there all the matches are getting completed and in a third day they waiting for results. One of his senior player starts a talk while they are in the lunch time it's about the transgenders and he asks his juniors to say their opinion about them, one of them says his opinion, he says I help them when I get anyone as a friend to me , and I shared their problems and sorrows with me if I'll be the district collector. His senior player congratulations him and after lunch it's the time to results for the matches his team won the runner up trophy and they leave there with a warm success then they wait for bus in a bus stand the boy who gave a speech about transgender holds the trophy in his hand a transgender came there and speaks with the players with a smile they enjoyed it and she asks the trophy for a view but his hands are buffering to give her the trophy And his senior player get the trophy from him and gave her she feels a good pleasure and returns to them and he make a look at the boy who gave the speech....

GNANA SEKARAN S

Gnana Sekaran S is a diploma mechanical engineer. He loves to write poetic lines. His Real life incidents and songs are his INSPIRATION. During school days his interest on elocution competition makes him to write quotes & poems. He loves music very much.

Instagram id; yours_lovingly_sekar

TRANSGENDER

SPECIAL PERSON !

The hormone changes,

Their battle begins...

Their identity changes,

Their soul begins...

They identify who they are,

They prove it WHAT THEY CAN DO...

IGNORING & HUMILATING never leave them,

LIKE FIGHTING & WINNING grow with them...

They are same as us,

More than strong then us...

No one will stop them,

Because they are special from god womb...

K. MONISHA

She is Monisha hails from Tamilnadu . She is passionate about her work and skills. Teacher in profession

TRANSGENDER

I seen transgender as same as all

I'm never feel her as different from us

There is no longer need to see her as abnormal

If proper opportunities gave to them

They will stand in brighter and huge position

PRIYA

She is priya from Tamilnadu. She is talkative and likes to share her feelings to others through words.

TRANSGENDER

Transgender don't need any pity

They need opportunity

They don't want attention

They want respect

Be a human

To treat everyone with

Dignity and equality.

I.K.HEMILAA

Hemilaa, a girl of 25 completed her master degree in English literature. Born in kovilpatti. A girl with dream become women with vision. She loves to write quotes, article stories. She is a lionhearted girl, wish to be " Hemilaa". " love is a key to success Spread love to everyone" Hemilaa

Instagram id ; Hemilaa_

GENDER EQUALITY

Birth to death
Through out their life
They face so many problem
Women is a queen
Men is a king
Transgender is a crowned head
They achieve in many field
Treat them equally
Gave respect to them and their feelings